IMAGES
of America

NEWARK

The Egyptian-style Essex County Courthouse, designed by John Haviland of Philadelphia, was used both as a Newark city hall and courthouse from 1838, when it was built, to 1848. A new courthouse was built behind it between 1903 and 1907, and this building was razed.

IMAGES
of America

NEWARK

Jean-Rae Turner and Richard T. Koles

ARCADIA

First published 1997
Copyright © Jean-Rae Turner and Richard T. Koles, 1997

ISBN 0-7524-0547-0

Published by Arcadia Publishing,
an imprint of the Chalford Publishing Corporation,
One Washington Center, Dover, New Hampshire 03820.
Printed in Great Britain

Library of Congress Cataloging-in-Publication Data applied for

Contents

Acknowledgments

We would like to express our sincere appreciation to the city's historian, Charles F. Cummings, who has provided photographs and information from his personal collection; Don Davidson, owner of New Jersey Newsphotos, for allowing us to select photos from his vast facilities and permitting us to use his office equipment; Barbara Moss, who assisted with the mechanics of the computer; Robert Blackwell, librarian in the New Jersey Information Center of the Newark Public Library, for reviewing the manuscript and photographs for accuracy; Valerie Austin and James Osbourn, also of the New Jersey Information Center, who have scurried around the many stacks, including library storage, for material; Dr. Alex Boyd, library director; Paul Pattwell, librarian; The Jewish Historical Society of MetroWest in Whippany and Joseph A. Settanni, the Society's archivist, and Saul Schwarz, a South Side or Shabazz High School graduate and authority about the Jewish presence in Newark; Howard Wiseman, a historian; Michael Yesenko, past president of both the Union County and Union Township Historical Societies; John Chance, Ruth Phair, and Edna Anselm, all members of the Victorian Society; John Cavicchia, a long-time friend and neighbor; Brother Augustine Curry, librarian at St. Benedict's Preparatory School; James Wright and his mother, Josephine Wright; Edward Bogle; Richard Grossklaus; Elizabeth Del Tufo; Mary Hill; Robert Kyber; William Gural; James Lowney; Russell Ogden; Olga Alvarez; Anthony Smith; John P. Shepherd Jr.; and all the others who assisted in this effort.

Introduction

This new graphic portrait of Newark, by Jean-Rae Turner and Richard T. Koles, is a refreshing view of New Jersey's largest city. It presents the viewer with many traditional panoramas, but it also contains photographs never before used in any publication, nor found in any public institution.

A careful search was made for illustrations in the New Jersey Information Center of the Newark Public Library and also in scrapbooks and private collections. The result is a publication of both old and new sources which will delight the reader. Here you will find churches, schools, houses, and parks, along with the people who worshiped, studied, lived, and played there during their lifetimes.

This new view of Newark was complied by two Newark natives. Jean-Rae Turner, a lifelong resident of the Weequahic section, has been a reporter for the *Elizabeth Daily Journal*, photographic librarian of the New Jersey Newsphotos, and author of a newspaper column and of several books. She brings to this book the concept of the historian recording her hometown.

Richard T. Koles, a photographer, was born in the Clinton Hill section and resided for many years in the Roseville section of Newark. Koles worked for Van Photos, which was under contract to the *Star-Ledger*, covering the Newark area. He also served as chief photographer at the *Elizabeth Daily Journal* before he became supervisor of the archives of New Jersey Newsphotos, contracted to do the photography for the *Star Ledger*. His contribution has been as a top drawer photojournalist who understands the city and is willing to share his knowledge with his viewers.

Newark's rich and varied past is thrown open to view in this deluxe graphic essay.

Charles F. Cummings
Newark City Historian
March 1997

This 40-foot long mural by C.Y. Turner in the 1906 Essex County Courthouse depicts the landing of the Puritans at the Landing Place on the Passaic River. It shows John Ward (the turner in the center) assisting Elizabeth Swaine ashore. They married and are the ancestors of many Newarkers.

One
A Puritan Village

The Settlers' Monument is an artist's version of the arrival of the first settlers from Milford, Connecticut, to the future Newark, led by Robert Treat in May 1666. The monument was erected at the Fairmount Cemetery in 1889, when these early settlers' bodies were moved from the old Burial Ground opposite the old First Presbyterian Church on Broad Street. Newark was initially called New Milford for Milford, Connecticut. The settlers also came from Guilford and Branford, Connecticut.

The Settlers' Monument in Fairmount Cemetery is 22 feet high. It stands on a granite base 8 feet square. The 7-foot high figure of the Puritan, manufactured in Bridgeport, Connecticut, is a metal structure painted gray to give it the appearance of stone. Some say the figure represents Robert Treat, leader of the first group of settlers.

The Puritans purchased the land from the Native Americans for gunpowder, bars of lead, axes, coats, guns, breeches, knives, hoes, wampum, and liquor. The plot of land extended from Bound Creek, along Newark Bay and the Passaic River, to Third River, and to the Watchung Mountains. The statue called *The Indian and the Puritan* (right) by Gutzon Borglum, the sculptor, was dedicated May 10, 1916, at Washington and Broad Streets. It is one of four statues by Borglum in Newark.

The Meeker homestead, built in 1678, stood at the intersection of Chancellor Avenue and Bergen Street until 1913, when the neighboring farms were subdivided for one-family houses in the Weequahic Section or South Ward. Chancellor Avenue originally was known as "Pot Pie Lane" because of the excellence of a resident's pies. The name was changed in honor of Chancellor Oliver Spencer Halsted, first chancellor of New Jersey. Halsted's farm was on the street.

The first one-room Lyons Farms School on the road to Elizabethtown (Elizabeth Avenue) at Pot Pie Lane was built in 1728. General George Washington led his troops past it on his famous retreat across New Jersey in 1776. The building was later burned during a raid by the British. In 1784, the farmers erected a brownstone building to replace it. The school was used until 1902. In 1938, it was moved to the walled garden of the Newark Museum at 49 Washington Street.

Rev. Abraham Pierson, a Congregational minister, served as pastor to the Newark colony. He renamed the new village Newark in honor of his native town Newark-On-Trent in England. He also established the church at Connecticut Farms (Union) in 1667. His statue is in the college yard at Yale University in New Haven, Connecticut. The church became Presbyterian when it joined the Presbytery of Philadelphia in 1717.

The first section of the Sydenham House was constructed about 1712, on the Old Road to Bloomfield. It is the oldest privately-owned dwelling in the city and has been owned by Mrs. Dorland J. Henderson and the late Mr. Henderson since 1954.

Rev. Aaron Burr Sr. resided in the manse for the old First Presbyterian Church while he was pastor of the church from 1737 to 1756. He also served as the second president of the College of New Jersey (later Princeton University) from 1747 to 1756, when he moved the college to Princeton with his wife, Esther Edwards, daughter of the well-known New England clergyman Rev. Jonathan Edwards, and their two children, Sally and Aaron Burr Jr.

Aaron Burr Jr., second vice-president of the United States, was born in the parsonage of the old First Presbyterian Church. A graduate of the College of New Jersey in 1772, he fought in the Revolutionary War. He met Alexander Hamilton in a duel in Weehawken in 1804 because he felt that Hamilton had hindered his advancement in politics. Hamilton was fatally wounded in the duel, and Burr's career declined. He was charged with treason, but not convicted. Burr spent the last years of his life on Staten Island.

Rev. Alexander Macwhorter, pastor of old First Presbyterian Church from 1759 to 1807, led opponents of the British during the war. When the British followed General Washington through the town in November 1776, Rev. Mr. Macwhorter had to flee. He sat with General George Washington at several of the general's council of war sessions.

The old First Presbyterian Church was badly damaged during the Revolutionary War. The church was rebuilt in 1791 from brownstone quarried in Newark. This church is considered to be the mother of most of the Presbyterian churches in the area of Essex and Passaic Counties.

This statue of General George Washington by W. Massey Rhind, placed in Washington Park, formerly known as the Old Market Place, in 1912, faces Broad Street and the route that General Washington took on his famous retreat in November 1776. He spent five days in Newark at that time. The tower of the American Insurance Company may be seen over his left shoulder. The building is now the Rutgers University Law School.

The home of New Jersey Superior Court Judge Elisha Boudinot was on Park Place until 1912. Washington attended the wedding of Boudinot and his bride, Catherine Smith, in Elizabethtown during the Revolutionary War. Boudinot was the younger brother of Elias Boudinot, president of the Continental Congress when the Treaty of Paris, which ended the war, was signed in 1783. Judge Boudinot was also president of the first bank, the Newark Banking and Insurance Company. The house was later razed to make room for the Public Service building.

Rev. Moses Combs is considered to be the father of Newark industry. He believed in the Puritan work ethic and became a shoemaker to participate in Newark's growing leather industry. He soon realized that his apprentices needed more instruction than what he was giving during the day, so he established a night school in 1790. Historians call the school Newark's first vocational school.

Sayres Coe, grandson of Benjamin Coe, the Pilgrim, lived in this attractive frame dwelling on Court Street and Coe Place. Newarkers believed that fences made good neighbors. The fences had a practical side too. Cattle, pigs, and sheep had to be fenced or they would eat vegetables in kitchen gardens. Coe's grandson, James, later moved to a High Street brownstone home.

Unlike the members of other churches in Newark, the people who founded the Lyons Farms Baptist Church in 1769 came overland from Piscataway and Scotch Plains to start this congregation. This nineteenth-century structure was the second for the church. Stones for the tiny graveyard are at the right. When the third and present building was erected in 1881, the graves were removed to Evergreen Cemetery in Lyons Farms. The church became the Elizabeth Avenue Baptist Church in 1913 and the Calvary Baptist Church in 1964.

Col. Josiah Ogden was a practical man in 1733. When his hay dried after a week of rain, he cut it despite the fact that it was the Lord's Day. Rebuked by Presbyterian church officials, he resigned and started a new church, the Trinity Episcopal Church, organized in 1746. The sanctuary was built on the Training Place (Military Park). Only the old tower remains of the original church, which was destroyed by fire in 1804 and rebuilt in 1810. The church became the Cathedral for the Newark Diocese in 1942. St. Philip's Episcopal Church, an African-American church on High Street at West Market Street, was destroyed by fire on December 20, 1964. The two churches united in 1966 and became Trinity and St. Philip's Cathedral in 1992.

Until Seth Boyden with his Yankee ingenuity settled in Newark in 1815, Newark had little manufacturing, although there were several craftsmen in the town. Boyden loved to solve problems. He developed a hide-splitting machine, a silver-plating process to prevent iron hardware from rusting, a machine to cut nails, patent leather, a process for making malleable iron, the area's first two steam locomotives for the Morris & Essex Railroad and the Essex and the Orange, and daguerreotypes. The statue (at left) by Karl Gerhardt is in Washington Park.

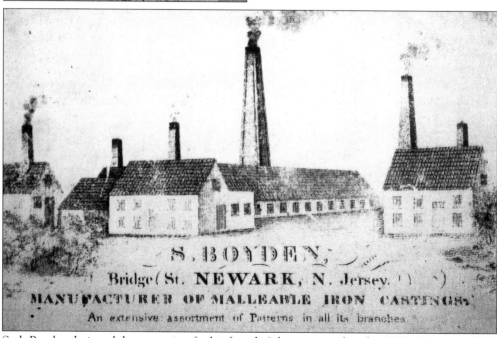

Seth Boyden designed the engraving for his foundry's business card in the 1830s. He successfully launched several successful industries as a result of his inventions, but sold them as he sought new ventures. He is credited with making Newark a diversified industrial city.

Two
Made in Newark

Newark began to grow as transportation improved. One the first improvements included a branch of the Morris Turnpike, known as the Springfield Turnpike, from Springfield to Newark (Springfield Avenue) in 1806. Other roads soon followed. The Morris Canal, chartered in 1824 and opened in 1832, brought boats loaded with coal, iron, wood, and vegetables. Newark was made a Port of Entry in 1835. The New Jersey Railroad and the Morris & Essex Railroad soon began operations, and Newark became a city in 1836. Lock 17 (above) was one of two locks on the 102-mile long Morris Canal in Newark. It was located on the present Lock Street, adjacent to the New Jersey Institute of Technology. The second lock was adjacent to the Passaic River.

N. J. DEMAREST & CO.,

MANUFACTURERS OF

Fine Single and Double

HARNESS,

243 & 245 MARKET STREET,

Near Mulberry St.,

NEWARK, N. J.

These are some of the advertisements in the Newark City Directory. The ads list a variety of the articles manufactured and sold in Newark.

SKINNER & LEARY,

Machinery in General,

5 and 7 RAILROAD PLACE. NEWARK, N. J

Stationary and Portable Steam Engines,

HOISTING & PILE DRIVING ENGINES, WITH FRICTIONAL GEARING.

DERRICKS AND CONTRACTORS' MACHINERY.

Freight and Passenger Elevators for Factories, Stores &c.

Shafting, Hangers, Pulleys, &c., constantly on hand or made to order.

GOODENOUGH
HAMMOCK COMPANY,

252 Market Street,

NEWARK, N. J.

MANUFACTURERS OF

COTTON, LINEN AND SILK HAMMOCKS

Our Hammocks are all made by hand, the mesh is small, and they are light and strong. We use only the best materials. All our goods are warranted. Tourists' Hammocks a specialty. We call especial attention to our Patented Hammock and Awning by means of which a perfect protection from the sun is had.

BRIC-A-BRAC.

MACRAME LACE.

Manufacturers and Exporters of Bric-a-Brac in Ebony, White Holly and Fancy Woods. Novelties in Wall Pockets, Brackets, Panels and Art Material.

SPECIAL ATTENTION GIVEN TO OUR EXPORT TRADE.

FACTORY,

252 MARKET STREET,

WM. E. GOODENOUGH. }
L. A. GOODENOUGH. } NEWARK, N. J., U.S.A.

The J.M. Quimby Carriage Company, started in 1834, was the one of the oldest in Newark. It joined the war effort during the Civil War, making field ambulances and gun carriages. After the automobile was invented, it began making bodies for them. When carriages became obsolete and automobile manufacturing moved to Michigan, the firm closed.

Employees of Theo. F. Johnson, Jacob Johnson Company, and Pioneer Mills, at 77–79 Mechanic Street (Edison Place), dealers in tea, coffee, and spices, are pictured standing in front of a wagon containing bags of spices. The street was renamed after Thomas A. Edison became famous. Edison's first factory was located on the street for five years, from 1871 to 1876. He later moved to Menlo Park and then to West Orange.

Wagons, such as this one, and carriages of all types were made in Newark, making the town one of the most important carriage and wagon manufacturers in New Jersey.

There were no zoning laws in Newark until well into the twentieth century. This meant that nice homes, such as this one pictured above, could easily be overwhelmed by a factory. However, sometimes the factory was operated by the owner of the house. C.R. Smith & Company and William F. Yeacen, manufacturers of metal plating, chromium, silver, nickel, and copper, were built around the house.

Two men are shown here working at machines in the Burstow Kollmar & Company, jewelers. Newark was a center of jewelry manufacturing. Among the manufacturers were Jacob Wiss and Company, scissor manufacturers who opened a jewelry store; George Krementz, who started Krementz & Co., which still exists in Newark; John Taylor and Colonel Isaac Baldwin, who formed Taylor and Baldwin in 1810; and James Madison Durand, who started Durand & Company in 1838. By 1874, there were more than fifty firms making jewelry in Newark. Henry Blank & Company, jeweler, joined the list of manufacturers at the turn of the century.

Phineas Jones and Company, makers of wheels and spokes, was located at 305 Market Street in 1915. Founded in Worcester, Massachusetts, in 1848, he moved briefly to Elizabeth, and then to Newark in 1860. The firm moved to Hillside about 1922 and made wheels for the Barnum and Bailey Circus. The company went bankrupt in 1924, after trucks replaced wagons.

In 1896, Tiffany & Company opened a plant in Newark which made sterling silver jewelry and also did silver plating. Here, P.E. Chance (to the right), a die cutter, works at a bench in the Tiffany plant. Chance, a native of Birmingham, England, came to this country in the 1880s. After the Tiffany plant closed, the huge castle-like building became a condominium and town-house development. Tiffany lamps and jewelry continue to be produced in other plants.

Farm girls and immigrants crowded into Weingarten's Corset Factory on High Street in 1905 to assemble the corsets which would give every woman an hourglass figure. Women frequently needed assistance to pull the strings on the corsets tight enough to achieve the dream of a perfect figure. Clothing factories such as these flourished as women ceased to make their own clothes or to have a dressmaker move in for a week or so to do the necessary sewing.

The Gottfried Krueger Brewing Company wagon was pulled by three dark horses, although many wagons only used two horses. The driver is E. Brasch and is accompanied by Tom Buechler, an employee for forty-two years. At that time, people often joined a company and stayed with it until they retired or died. Other breweries in the city included those owned by Christian Feigenspan, Peter Ballantine, George H. Wiedenmayer, Joseph Hensler, the Schalk Brothers, Lorenz & Jacquillard, and others. Only one brewery remains today. Anheuser Busch Inc. of St. Louis, Missouri, built a huge complex in Newark in 1950.

George J. Busch, the proprietor of a shop for watches and jewelry, claimed to be Newark's oldest jeweler when he was located in this store on High Street and Springfield Avenue in 1882. Busch also guaranteed his watches for one year.

The Cathedral of the Sacred Heart, on the edge of Branch Brook Park, took fifty-six years to build, from 1898 to 1954. Jeremiah O'Rouke, who also designed St. James Roman Catholic Church, was the initial architect for this cathedral, one of the largest in the nation. It is considered to be one of the best examples of French Gothic architecture. The cathedral has eight chapels and two hundred windows, including a Rose window. It replaced St. Patrick's Pro-Cathedral for the Archdiocese of Newark. Sacred Heart is listed on the National Register of Historic Places. Pope John Paul II designated it as a basilica after his visit in October 1995.

Three
City of Churches

This is a bird's-eye view of Trinity Cathedral, the seat of the Episcopal Diocese of Newark and now known as Trinity and St. Philip's Cathedral. It is on an acre of ground adjacent to Military Park. The building at the extreme right is a dwelling which became the site for the Newark Athletic Club. To the left of that is the Military Park Hotel, and next to the hotel is the Firemen's Insurance Company building. The insurance company building has been expanded and remodeled. The others have been removed to make room for the New Jersey Performing Arts Center.

The old First Baptist Church, formed by the Lyons Farms Baptist Church, stood at 25 Academy Street at the corner of Halsey Street in 1855. The building was erected in 1810 and enlarged in 1841. A new church for the congregation was built on Broad Street in 1860. It continues to serve today as the Peddie Memorial Baptist Church, named for T.B. Peddie, a Newark merchant who endowed the church.

St. Benedict's College was founded by Benedictine monks from Germany in 1868. St. Mary's Roman Catholic Church, now St. Mary's Abbey, is at the right. The college, which ceased operation during World War I, also conducted a preparatory school. This school continued to flourish, serving German, Irish, and Italian Roman Catholics until the Newark riot in July 1967 and the white flight from the city which followed it. St. Benedict's Preparatory School closed in 1972. The Benedictine monks who remained were determined to continue serving the city. In 1973, the school reopened with black and Hispanic students who have proven they too can succeed in academia and on the athletic field.

The cornerstone of the new DeGroot Methodist Episcopal Church was dedicated in 1911. The DeGroot congregation was formed in 1864, and the final service was conducted in 1950. There were twelve Methodist churches in Newark in the 1920s. However, only four remain today.

The DeGroot Methodist Episcopal Church on South Orange and Littleton Avenues became the Chapel in the Woods, and then the Bergen Street Chapel. Many of the churches and synagogues in the city have changed denominations, but they continue to be used for religious purposes.

German Jews settled in the city about the same time as other German immigrants. The first congregation was B'nai Jeshurun, organized on August 20, 1848. The temple was built on the corner of Washington and William Streets in 1858. It became the largest synagogue in the city.

The Oheb Shalom Congregation split from B'nai Jeshurun in 1860 to form a new body, and a synagogue was built on Prince Street. The building, the oldest synagogue still standing in the city, was used for many years by the Metropolitan Baptist Church until a new sanctuary was built for them. The structure is being restored for use by the Newark Conservancy and is on the National Register of Historic Places.

Rabbi Moshe Feinstein is one of the many rabbis who has served Newark congregations. At one time, the city boasted fifty-three synagogues, although now there are only two left. One of the synagogues left is located in the Vailsburg section, and the other is on Broadway Street. The others that still exist have moved out of the city.

One of the best known rabbis in Newark was Rabbi Joachim Prinz, spiritual leader of the Temple B'nai Abraham for many years. The congregation, originally composed of Polish Jews, was organized in 1853.

The St. Dominic Monastery is a definite rarity in the United States. It is a community of cloistered nuns, who reside behind a walled nunnery on 13th Avenue at South 10th Street. The order, founded in Spain in the thirteenth century, has been located in Newark since 1880.

The North Reformed Church on Broad Street, designed by architect William H. Kirk, was built in 1859, for a three-year-old congregation. The church was badly damaged by fires in 1922 and 1931, but was later restored.

With its two matching towers, St. Paul's Methodist Episcopal Church at Broad and Marshall Streets was one of the most spectacular sanctuaries in the city. A new church was built on Mount Prospect and Grafton Avenues when the congregation moved to the North Ward. This building was used by the Downtown Boys' Club for eighteen years before it was torn down in 1936.

The Queen of Angels Roman Catholic Church was formed in 1930 for the growing African-American Roman Catholic population, which previously had no church of its own. Rev. William Linder, pastor during the Newark riots of 1967, conducted a survey of the congregation to discover members' needs, and then formed New Community Corporation (NCC) to meet them. NCC has daycare centers, senior and low-cost housing, a nursing home, and shopping area.

Rev. James Roosevelt Bayley was a descendant of Nicholas Roosevelt, a cousin of two American presidents, and a nephew of Mother Seton. He was named Bishop of Newark in 1853 and selected St. Patrick's Roman Catholic Church, dedicated on St. Patrick's Day in 1850, as his cathedral. It became known as St. Patrick's Pro-Cathedral.

St. Patrick's Pro-Cathedral was the third Roman Catholic church to be built in Newark. St. John's Church on Mulberry Street and St. Mary's on High Street were the first and second respectively. St. John's, near the Penn Station (New Jersey Transit), serves a large commuter congregation. St. Mary's, now St. Mary's Abbey, is part of the St. Benedict's complex.

Rev. Aloysius Gorman, seated center, continues to read while his fellow monks pose for this photograph at St. Mary's Benedictine Priority. Standing are (left to right) Rev. Julian Kilger, Rev. Alexander Reger, Rev. Bonaventure Ostendarp, and Rev. Anthony Wirtner. Seated are (left to right) Very Rev. Gerald Pilz, Rev. Fred Hoesel, Rev. Brother Gorman, Rev. Fridolin Meyer, and Rev. Albert Robrecht.

Rev. Ambrose Huebner is honored as the oldest monk in the Benedictine Order in 1932. He was eighty-four years old at the time. A native of Down Neck, as the Ironbound was originally known, he attended St. James School and was confirmed by Bishop James Roosevelt Bayley. He was ordained in 1872.

The Very Right Rev. Abbot Ernest Helmstetter, O.S.B., was president of St. Benedict's and director of St. Mary's Abbey and St. Benedict's College from 1888 to 1913.

Rev. James Aloupis, pastor of St. Nicholas Greek Orthodox Church; his daughter (left), Miss Constance Aloupis; and his wife (right), Mrs. Georgia Aloupis, welcome guests at the eighty-fifth anniversary ball of the church at the Landmark Inn, Woodbridge, on February 21, 1987.

Rev. Arthur Northwood, D.D., was pastor of the Elizabeth Avenue Presbyterian Church, originally the Lyons Farms Presbyterian Church, from 1920 to 1960. He served as moderator of the Newark Presbytery from 1928 to 1929, and the Synod of New Jersey from 1952 to 1953. He was also president of the South Newark Ministerial Association in 1927.

Archbishop Thomas E. Boland of the Diocese of Newark (on the right) celebrates the fiftieth anniversary of his ordination on May 31, 1972, at the Cathedral of the Sacred Heart.

The control tower of the Newark Airport, Newark's second airfield, stands beside one of the runways. Begun in 1928, the airport received a United States mail contract and soon became one of the busiest fields in the nation. In 1942, the airport was taken over by the federal government for the war effort. In 1948, it was leased to the Port Authority of New York, now called the Port Authority of New Jersey and New York. International service began in 1989.

Four
The Hub

Newark Bay and the Passaic River brought settlers and products to Newark and gave Newarkers easy access to other ports. When railroads began pushing through the town in the 1830s, people and freight could be carried in all directions, making Newark the hub of commerce and pleasure. The Pennsylvania Railroad Bridge (in the foreground) and the Jackson Street Bridge carry trains and vehicles across the Passaic River to Harrison, while a tug boat guides a ship between the two bridges.

Mayor Jerome T. Congleton (1928–1933) puts the first mailbag on an airplane at the Newark Airport in 1928 after the city was awarded a contract by the United States Postal Service.

This Pennsylvania Railroad Station on Market Street sported impressive turrets. The second to serve the city, it was replaced in the 1930s by the present station.

The Delaware, Lackawanna, and Western Railroad Station has changed very little since this photo was taken *c.* 1900. Now operated by the New Jersey Transit, the station serves a large commuter population.

The Eagle Rock Trolley number 351, owned by the Public Service Transport, travels along a Newark street in 1924. After the blizzard of 1888, overhead electric wires for trolley cars were placed underground. It was 1946 before all the wires in the Newark area were out of the way.

Individual bus lines were started in the second decade of the twentieth century by enterprising men. By 1926, all the lines had been purchased by Public Service Transport, now New Jersey Transit. This bus served North Newark. Buses quickly replaced the electric trolley cars in the 1920s.

In this photograph, a passenger train passes the second Pennsylvania Station. Note that the tracks have been elevated; originally they were at street level.

A tugboat is pictured at the dock of the
Newark Lime Cement Company, c. 1916.

These ships are being loaded with foodstuffs for Russian relief at Newark on April 11, 1922.
Port Newark was leased to the Port Authority in 1948 and has since become the busiest in the
New York area. It is also the second largest container port in the United States. Only Long
Beach, California, is bigger.

The old Morris Canal bed stretching from Newark Penn Station to Belleville became the Newark City Subway, while the street became Raymond Boulevard, named for the popular Mayor Thomas Lynch Raymond. Both the subway and the boulevard helped to move people out of the crowded Newark streets. The subway later became part of the New Jersey Transit system. The murals showing people working are displayed at four stations.

A trolley car emerges from a tunnel in Newark in 1916.

The "Four Corners," as the intersection of Broad and Market Streets is called, was once considered the busiest in the world. Note the traffic islands for the trolley cars. The police tower which stood at the spot from 1922 to 1939 is behind the front trolley car. Unlike those in many other eastern cities, Broad Street really is broad. The settlers made it 132 feet wide. Public areas were placed in the middle and at either end. They are now Military, Washington, and Lincoln Parks.

Newark had many piano companies, where such brands as Steger Pianos were made and sold. Pianos were one of the chief instruments of entertainment. Nearly every child took piano lessons, and evening songfests around the piano were very common.

Long before Gutzon Borglum carved presidents' faces on Mount Rushmore, South Dakota, he did four sculptures in downtown Newark which have been listed on the New Jersey Register of Historic Places. The *Wars of America* (above) statue in Military Park depicts figures which represent all the wars the United States participated, from the Revolutionary War through World War I. The other statues are *The Landing Place Monument*, which is being restored in the new New Jersey Performing Arts Complex, *The Seated Lincoln* located in front of the Essex County Courthouse, and *The Indian and the Puritan* in Washington Park.

Five

They Serve

Posters such as this offered bonuses to men who desired to join the army during the Civil War. Each captain formed his own company usually from a single community. A $100 bonus was offered for Captain Pennington's Company.

General Philip Kearny, the one-armed hero from Newark in the Civil War, visited his grandparents in this cottage on Belleville Avenue (Broadway). He commanded the Second Regiment in the Peninsula Campaign until he was killed September 1, 1862. The cottage site became the location for the Newark Normal School in 1913. The school later became a college. It moved to the Hamilton Fish Kean Estate in Union Township in 1958. The name was changed to Kean College.

The white home of Governor Marcus Ward (above left) stood on Washington Street at the time of the Civil War. The local military hospital was named for him. The two mansions just beyond his house were owned by the Ballantine family. The first building on the right with the tower is the Second Presbyterian Church, which was called "The Blue Church" because of the color of its stone. Later, this church was replaced, but then the new building burned. The church's latest replacement was closed in 1996. The sanctuary is currently being used by the Central Presbyterian Church.

Mrs. Ellen Bogle, a native of County Cork, Ireland, worked as a domestic at the White House in Washington, D.C. during the Civil War. In an interview with a local newspaper in 1931, she recalled that the White House gates were locked at 10 pm. She gained nocturnal freedom by talking with the guards and finally marrying one of them, who was named Thomas Bogle. He served in the Union Army. At war's end, they relocated in the Ironbound Section of Newark (the East Ward). Like many Irish girls, Mrs. Bogle came to this country alone and then found a husband.

The statue of the seated Abraham Lincoln by Gutzon Borglum is in front of the Essex County Courthouse. Children love to sit on the statue's lap.

The Fairmount Cemetery donated a plot of land for free graves for men who served in the Civil War. The tall column is topped by a figure of a Civil War soldier. Government markers are on the grave of each man.

Robert Bogle is dressed in his Spanish-American War uniform as he poses for a photograph with his wife, Josephine.

The *Newark Daily Advertiser* (right) began publishing in 1832 as the city's first daily newspaper. It continued to publish until 1906. The publisher changed the name to the *Newark Star*, which later became the *Newark Star-Eagle* and finally the *Star Ledger*.

The *Morning Register*, another newspaper, shared a building with the Temperance House. It is one of the seventeen Newark newspapers that are predecessors to the *Star-Ledger*.

Frank Calabrese served with the United States Army during World War II. After the war, he became a draftsman with Frank Grad & Sons, one of the city's outstanding architectural firms. Nearly every family was touched by the war.

This is a photograph of young men lining up at a draft board in Newark.

Michael Yesenko, a student at Weequahic High School, quit school with three buddies to join the United States Army. He smiles proudly in his uniform at a local photo studio in November 1946 before leaving to serve with the army of occupation at Beppu, Japan, with the 19th Infantry Regiment, 24th Infantry Division. When he returned home, he used the G.I. Bill to earn a college degree and become chairman of the history department at Union High School, Union Township.

A cross monument honoring Rev. John Washington, a Newark native, stands on the lawn of St. Rose of Lima R.C. Church on Orange Street. Father Washington was baptized, received his first communion, was confirmed, and celebrated his first Mass at the church. He was one of the four chaplains on the *U.S.S. Dorchester*, a troop carrier, when it sank on February 3, 1943, in the Atlantic Ocean after being torpedoed by the Germans. The chaplains gave their life jackets to servicemen on the sinking ship, then joined hands in prayer, and went down with the ship.

Jerome N. "Jerry" Waldor enlisted in the United States Navy after graduating from Weequahic High School in January 1945. He earned an appointment to the United States Military Academy at West Point, New York, graduating in 1950. He served five years active duty with the air force and thirty-five years with the air force reserve. When he was honorably discharged in 1987, he held the rank of major general. He is president of Brounell, Kramer, Waldor, Kane Agency in Union.

Mary and Edward Hill, a sergeant in the United States Air Force, are photographed here shortly after they were married during World War II.

PFC Louis Schleifer (United States Army Air Corps) was one of four servicemen from Newark killed on December 7, 1941, in the Japanese attack on Pearl Harbor. He stood on the runway at Hickam Field firing his service revolver at the planes until he was killed. The Jewish War Veterans placed a memorial fountain in Milford Park in his honor. The park's name was changed to Schleifer Park. A poem he wrote is on the fountain. The others, who were killed, were all on ships. They included Archie Callahan Jr., a mess attendant on the *Oklahoma*, for whom a park also is named; Raymond Kerrigan, a machinist's mate, on the *Vestal*; and Nicholas Runiak, a seaman on the *Arizona*, for whom Kerrigan and Runiak Streets are named.

Technical Sergeant Joseph Koles (U.S. Army) and his brother, Pharmacist's Mate Richard T. Koles (U.S. Navy) met at Fort Bragg, North Carolina in 1946, after Sergeant Koles returned from the European Theater, where he participated in the Battle of the Bulge and V.E.-Day with the 82nd Airborne. Sergeant Koles became a chemist with the United States Treasury Department, and Pharmacist's Mate Koles became a news photographer.

Neither snow nor dark of night prevented Fire Engine No. 3 from responding to a fire in 1906.

This hand-drawn hose cart is the oldest piece of equipment at the Newark Fire Museum in the carriage house of the Newark Museum at 49 Washington Street. The carriage house once was used to house the carriages of Governor Marcus Ward.

Two white horses pull Engine Company 3 in 1896.

Ten years later, Engine Company Number 3 is being pulled by three horses, as it travels down Court Street.

Firemen fight a blaze in the Newark Hardware Company on Springfield Avenue in 1920.

Members of Engine Company No. 14 crowd on the hose wagon at the company's headquarters on McWhorter and Vesey Streets. The wagon, a Amoskeag Steamer, was put into service in 1897 and was used until 1903.

Firemen from Engine Company No. 6 line up in front of the steamer they called "Mount Pelee." It was named after the volcano of the same name because of the sparks that flew out of it as it traveled along the street. The firehouse was located on Springfield Avenue between Morris and Bergen Streets in 1894.

This firehouse for Hook and Ladder Company No. 1 and Engine Company No. 1 stood on Broad Street opposite the old First Presbyterian Church. The old burial ground of the church may be seen through the center arch. The building was demolished when Branford Place was cut through in 1889.

Members of old Third Precinct line up for inspection at the headquarters in 1907.

Several small children stand on the curb to admire the Sixth Precinct's new patrol wagon in 1913. It was a six-cylinder Kline vehicle with oil lamps mounted on the sides. Peter Pfrommer, a sergeant in the Fourth Precinct, is the driver. Note that the steering wheel is on the right instead of the left side.

Theodore Bauer was the first mounted police officer in the city in 1891. His horse was owned by Jacob Haussling. Bauer retired in 1911. The police department continues to have a squad of mounted policemen.

A police officer in 1930 models a 1900 uniform.

The bicycle patrol poses for this 1890 photograph.

Two patrolmen armed with machine guns stand in front of the first radio patrol car, a Ford. The two officers are wearing different trousers and shoes. The one at the left is dressed to ride a motorcycle, and the officer on the right is dressed for foot patrol.

Officer Patrick Tuite sits proudly on his mount as Police Director William J. Egan (left) and Police Captain Matthew J. Bolger inspect the horse.

Patrolman Charles Keepers directs traffic in 1925, using both a sign and his hand. He is standing on a small wooden platform.

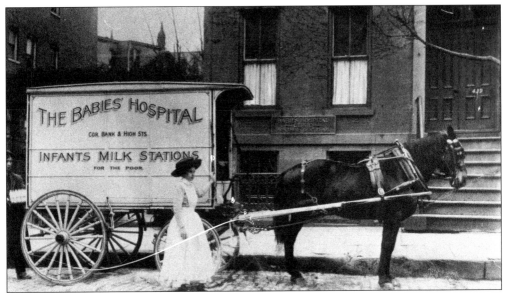

An infants' milk station for the poor was conducted at the Babies' Hospital on Bank and High Streets. Dr. Henry L. Coit was one of the founders of the hospital in 1896. He spearheaded a drive to provide purified milk. The first bottle of certified milk was delivered to him in May 1893.

The Presbyterian Hospital became part of United Hospitals. Each ethnic or religious group formed its own hospitals to care for the sick. One of the hospitals was the German Hospital, where Clara Maass received her training. After her death of malaria during the Spanish-American War, the hospital was renamed for her. It later moved to Belleville. The Kenney Hospital, opened in 1924 by Dr. John A. Kenney and later called the Community Hospital, was the first and only African-American hospital in the city. It closed in 1953. St. James Hospital, St. Michael's Hospital, Columbus Hospital, The American Legion Hospital, and the City Hospital are just a few of the others..

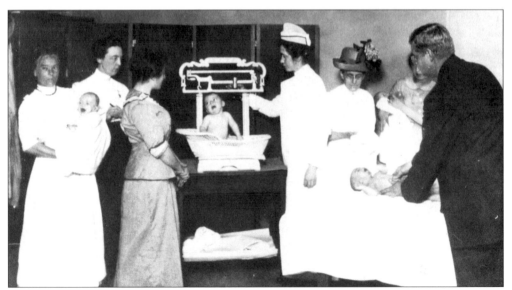

Dr. Henry L. Coit (on right) examines a baby in the Baby Keep Well Station, c. 1896. He encouraged mothers to bring their babies to the stations for regular check-ups to prevent disease. This was before all children were immunized against various childhood diseases and when infant mortality was still very high.

Louise Arcularius poses for this picture in her nurse's uniform.

The Center Street Hospital (shown here in a drawing) is one of many small hospitals which were operated in the city. Others included an insane asylum, homeopathic hospital, St. Barnabas Hospital, and the Eye and Ear Infirmary.

The Beth Israel Hospital was organized in 1901, in a mansion on High Street (Martin Luther King Boulevard). By 1908, a new larger facility was open nearby on High Street at West Kinney Street. It grew fast and was soon overcrowded. Within twenty years, a larger facility was open on Osborne Terrace and Lyons Avenue in the Weequahic Section (South Ward). Lyons Avenue and Chancellor Avenue became doctors' rows as physicians conducted their practices from their homes. The hospital now is part of the St. Barnabas Health Care System.

Six

Three R's

The Newark Public Library opened in 1901 at 5 Washington Street. Note the traffic island for a police officer in the center of the street. *The Indian and the Puritan* statue is at the left of the photograph. The statue was erected in 1916. The library has long been considered one of the best in New Jersey, and its New Jersey Information Center is a main depository of information on the state.

Dr. E.O. Hovey was the first principal of the Newark High School, the city's first secondary school, from 1872 to 1899. The school later became Barringer High School, named for the city's first superintendent of schools, William Barringer.

Girls in an unidentified school participate in a sewing class at their regular classroom desks.

The teaching staff of the Beacon Street German American School in 1877, from left to right, included (standing) Mr. Grossmann, Arnold Voget, and Mr. Oches; (sitting) Miss Lawrence, Mrs. Meeker, Miss Malerand, and Miss Modcer. There were few jobs for women in those days, although teaching was an approved occupation. Except for widows, it was unusual to have a married woman teacher.

J. Ward Smith (center) was the principal of the 18th Avenue School in 1880 and is pictured here with his school's faculty.

Eli Pickwick Jr. was the first principal of East Side High School. He served from 1913, when the school opened, until he retired in 1933.

Arthur Vincent Taylor was a Latin teacher at Barringer High School, Newark, for forty-seven years.

James Baxter was requested to come to
Newark after the Civil War to head the
Colored School on Market Street. He gained
the respect of Newarkers when he demanded
excellence of his pupils and their admission to
the high school. When he retired in 1909, the
school was closed and African-Americans
were welcomed in the public schools.

This is a sewing class in 1930 in the Essex
County Girls Vocational School. The school
opened in 1928.

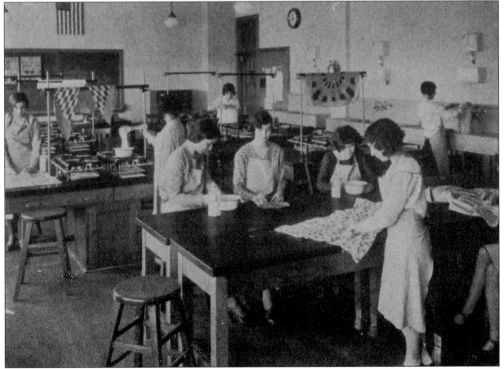

Essex County College was founded in 1966. It opened in September 1968 in the Essex Building at 31 Clinton Street, Newark. In 1970, the college purchased 11 acres from the Newark Housing Authority for its campus in the University Heights section. In 1985, the West Essex campus in West Caldwell was purchased from the West Essex Extension Center.

The Class of 1932 at Blessed Sacrament School poses for its class picture.

The Class of 1934 at Maple Avenue School is photographed in front of the school. Most of the children in the class were Jewish. The Weequahic Section had a large Jewish population for nearly forty years, and sociologists have done case studies on the area.

The Drake College was at 728 Broad Street in 1900, above the law offices of Atwater and Carter on the first floor. Note the clock over the door. The college was one of many specialized schools in the city.

Young women at the Fawcett School of Art, later known as the Newark School of Fine and Industrial Arts, work in a classroom. Many artists learned their skills in the school.

In this c. 1930 photograph, each girl in the cooking class at the Essex County Girls Vocational School had her own work station.

A small boy (pictured on the left) pushes buttons on a permanent display of motion at the Newark Museum in the early 1960s.

A public drinking fountain, featuring delicate Gothic stone tracery, stood at the corner of the 1892 Prudential Insurance Company building on Bank and Broad Streets. It was moved to the walled garden of the Newark Museum in the 1950s when the Prudential building was razed.

The Newark Museum (on the left) and the home of John Ballantine, now a part of the museum, are located on Washington Street.

Here, Agnes Carus sits with two children. Note the lace collars. Many women made their own lace for clothes, curtains, and bed linens.

Seven
Life in the City

The Coe children pose in front of their High Street family home before taking a ride in their goat cart, c. 1885. They are (from left to right) Laura Mabel, Helen Augusta, Anna Florence, James D., Frederick, and in the baby carriage, Roland B. Coe. Mr. and Mrs. James A. Coe stand inside the fence, while the coachman's son holds the goats. Standing with the carriage is the baby's nurse.

Jennie Anselm and her two children, Florence and Paul, sit on a rock during a family outing. Each Sunday the family visited a Newark park.

Joseph and Julia Koleszar and their children, Wilma (on the left) and Joseph, pose for a photograph, c. 1900. Mr. Koleszar, an employee of the Westinghouse Corporation, held several patents.

In 1901, Helen Augusta Coe wore this white-dotted Swiss gown with pink ribbons and a pink and black hat when she served as a bridesmaid at the wedding of her sister, Anna Florence, and Robert N. Brockway, at the High Street Presbyterian Church nearby. The church is now St. James African Methodist Episcopal Church.

Pasquale Amato (who was called Pat) and Vincenza Amato (who was known as Jenny) have a formal photograph taken after their wedding.

Little Helen Irene Howard holds onto a chair for support, *c*. 1897.

Marie Hake features a little curl right in the middle of her forehead, *c*. 1901.

Frank Howard Jr. (1888–1920) is pictured here wearing a large bow tie. He died of injuries suffered on May 12, 1920, when an acetylene gas tank exploded at the Prest-O-Lite Company at Doremus Avenue and Avenue B.

Bobby Faraher balances himself on a chair as he puts one leg through the armrest. Faraher grew up to become a United States Navy pilot in World War II. He suffered from cancer and died before the war ended.

Mr. and Mrs. Frank M. Howard took their hats off for this photo in July 1886.

Louis Anselm holds his rifle as his
Grandmother Radenheimer holds him in
this photograph.

Julia Golembuski stands with her
brother in this 1888 portrait.

Angelo Cavicchia and his four brothers were shepherds in Italy in the 1880s, when they lost most of their sheep during a cold winter. They went to France in search of work, found none, and came to the United States. Angelo settled in Newark's Ironbound. His descendants include educators, ministers, a special agent in charge of the United States Secret Service Office, a congressman, and an assembly speaker.

Arthur V. Taylor (on the left) and a friend pause for a moment while on a bicycle ride. Bicycles were very popular in the 1880s and 1890s. Note that both men are well dressed for their riding excursion.

Elsie Oschwald poses for this photograph in 1910. Large hats and puffed sleeves were in vogue at the time.

Assunta Molinari (who was called Sue by her family and friends) poses for a portrait before participating in a wedding.

The Armm brothers, whose father operated the first kosher restaurant in Newark, are all dressed alike in this photograph. The youngest is dressed in a skirt. Baby boys and girls alike wore long skirts in the 1890s.

This *c.* 1923 photograph shows the Krasner family. Standing in the rear is Abraham, a local merchant. From left to right in the front is Louis, Bertha, baby Jacob (Jack) on his mother's lap, Lena (the wife and mother), and Helen.

Joseph Hankewich holds a candle used in his confirmation, c. 1923.

Elsie and Loretta Kolb participate in their first communions.

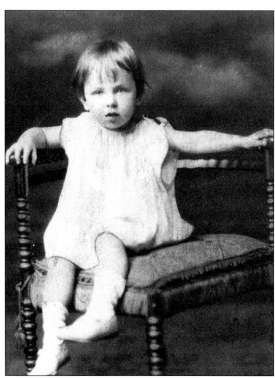

Nora Catherine McKinley sits on a reception chair, which has only one arm and a back. This style of chair was once extremely popular.

Ludwina Weiss Yesenko places protective hands on her daughters, Mary (five years old, on the left) and Matilda (three years old) *c.* 1920.

Eliza Dole grew up in Newark but later moved to Portland, Oregon. Her sisters, en route to visit her, were among the first people to sail through the Panama Canal after it opened.

Raffella Pellechia Del Tufo prepares for her wedding. She was the mother of Raymond Del Tufo, who served as a district court judge and United States attorney for New Jersey, and Robert J. Del Tufo, who was a state attorney general and United States attorney for New Jersey.

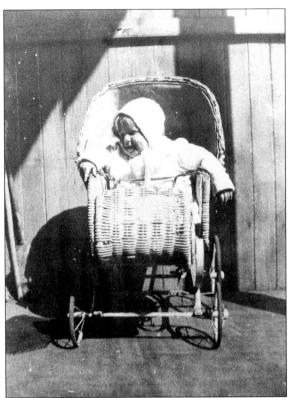

Wicker baby carriages were once especially popular, along with wicker furniture. In these two photographs, two babies are ready for outings. Jean-Rae Turner (pictured on left) is in the yard of the family home on High Street. Note the board fence that separates the yards.

Florence Anselm takes in the fresh air in her wicker carriage.

Jessie MacRae, a teacher, sits in an occasional chair. She was a volunteer serving on committees that organized Parent-Teachers Associations, League of Women Voters, and an adult school. She also collected for the Community Chest, sang in her church choir and the Festival Chorus, served as an air raid warden in World War II, and taught Sunday school.

William R. Turner, a mechanical engineer, became plant engineer of the roll celluloid department of the Celluloid Company, later the Celanese Corporation of America. He was later made plant manager.

LEFT: Maria Louise Bockel (1855–1923) purchased houses next to new schools in growing neighborhoods. When the schools needed additional classrooms, she sold her houses to them. When she died she left more than two million dollars to her children.

BOTTOM LEFT: Theodore F. Keer (bottom left picture) made more than sixteen trips to Europe before World War I to purchase paintings for the family art store opposite the city hall. After his marriage, he moved to the Forest Hill section of Newark. Keer later became a partner in the insurance agency of Van Vliet and Keer. Their office was on the second floor of the Prudential Insurance Company building on Broad Street.

BOTTOM RIGHT: Profile photographs were popular when this picture was taken of Ethel MacRae (bottom right) in 1916. She moved to the Forest Hill section of Newark after her marriage.

Josephine Kolb had Mary Pickford
curls in this portrait.

Marion Holgate, a Newark teacher, poses
for a wedding photo in 1927.

Elizabeth Travosano Molinari, the mother of eleven children, operated a greengrocery in North Newark.

Dr. Charles J. Caspar practiced on Broad Street from the 1920s to the 1960s. He is pictured with his wife, Josephine.

William Gural rests his arm on a bench in this 1920 picture. He joined the United States Navy and served during World War II. He also served as mayor of Hillside Township and later as a deputy attorney general for the State of New Jersey.

Joseph Bakes smiles in his high school yearbook picture. Joseph was a member of the Class of 1967 at Essex County Catholic High School, located in the old Mutual Benefit building on Broadway. He became a reporter and is now bureau chief of the Somerset Office of the *Star Ledger*, the state's largest newspaper.

A woman pushes a baby carriage across the bumpy cobblestones of the street beside the Newark Shoe Bazaar. Notice that the word "bazaar" is spelled incorrectly.

A wooden fireman, hand-carved by John Campbell of Belleville, stands atop the Firemen's Insurance Company building at Broad and Market Streets. The company was founded in 1810. This ornate building was erected in 1868 and was demolished for a new structure in 1909.

Eight

Commerce

Many newspapers were published in Newark in the nineteenth century. Of these, seventeen were the forerunners of the *Star Ledger*. The *Sunday Standard* was one of those ancestors.

Until Louis Bamberger (left), came to Newark and started L. Bamberger & Company, the city contained many small speciality stores dealing only in a single product. Bamberger, L.S. Plaut, and Hahne's changed the way Newarkers shopped by offering a wide variety of products. People from all over New Jersey came to the stores.

Bamberger's windows displayed a wide variety of their clothes and furniture in the 1930s. People flocked to the store for lunch, fashion shows, bargains, or to meet friends.

This ornate Victorian structure
housed the Mutual Benefit Life
Insurance Company.

The *Newark Evening News*, founded in 1883
by Wallace M. Scudder, quickly became the
state's largest newspaper, until the 1970s.

The Kresge Department Store replaced L.S. Plaut & Company, known as "The Bee Hive Store," on Broad Street in the early 1920s. A tiny portion of the Morris Canal may be seen at the left, where it went underground to the Passaic River. Both stores were major department stores in the city.

Gosdorfer's offered great sales on clothing. The sign on the corner is an advertisement for the Empire Theater. Newark had many theaters.

A horse-drawn carriage stops in front of Healy & Bogert Tailors. Heath and Drake, a carpet store, is located in the Heath building, to the left.

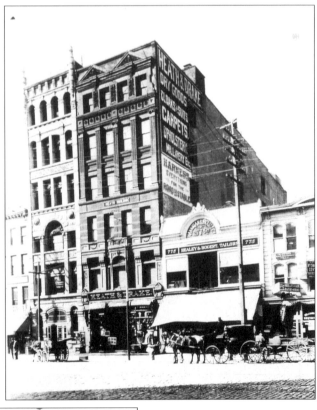

The Lauter Piano Company and Eisele's Shoes are close to the Arcade, the tallest building to the right. The Arcade, located on Broad Street, could be considered the first Newark shopping mall, since it housed a variety of small shops.

Hahne & Company is decorated for Christmas with a wreath and American flags. The store was the oldest department store in the city. It opened in 1858.

Anthony Smith (left) dared to start his own business in 1932, when he opened this gasoline station on 13th Avenue just above the Essex County Courthouse. Leonard S. Coleman Sr. (at far right) is wearing a money changer. Coleman's son, Leonard Jr., served as Commissioner of Energy and Community Affairs under New Jersey Governor Thomas Kean and is president of the National Baseball League. The other two men in the photograph are unidentified. Smith's grandsons now operate the successful business.

In the 1890s, Samuel Armm opened the first kosher restaurant in Newark. The restaurant was located on High Street, between Court Street and Mercer Street.

Small businesses dot this street. I.W. Bonnell, grocer and tea merchant, is at the left, while the Conger Insurance Company has a banner hanging over the sidewalk and a sign over the front door, not unlike some businesses do today.

Helen Cole and Ruth Freckleton of East Side High School won the Class B Junior Championship in the Essex County Women's Tennis Tourney in 1923. The championship was held at the Essex County Country Club.

Amusement parks, such as the Electric Park in the Vailsburg section of the city (pictured above), were favorite places of entertainment in warm weather. Dreamland, on the Newark-Elizabeth line, and Olympic Park, just outside the city in Irvington, were also popular places for Newark citizens to visit.

Nine
Recreation

In this photograph, boys are playing baseball in a stadium put up by Wiedenmayer's Brewery. The "beer barons," as they were called, contributed much to the city and also built beautiful mansions in the area. Three of those mansions, the Ballantine Mansion, the Krueger Mansion, and the Feigenspan Mansion, still stand today. The first two homes are owned by the city and are being restored.

The Newark Little Giants pose for this picture before a game in 1886. Newark had many baseball and softball teams. Every vacant lot offered possibilities as an unofficial ball field.

Everett Marcelle (on the left) was a catcher for the Newark Eagles in the late 1940s, before African-Americans played on the white professional ball teams.

Jimmie Hill, the Newark Eagles pitcher, was known as "Mr. Five by Five." Here, he pitches a ball at the Ruppert Stadium. The stadium was also used for stock car races in the 1950s.

Kathleen Keer (left) rides a homemade seesaw on a lot between Grumman and Keer Avenues after the farmland was sub-divided for new houses. Keer Avenue was named for her family. The girls are holding flags in observance of Decoration Day, as Memorial Day was once known.

The championship basketball team from the Morton Street School records their victory with a team portrait for the 1913–1914 season.

A golfer putts at the Forest Hill Golf Club.

Sulkies round a bend on the track at the old Waverly Fair Grounds. Weequahic Park, one of the two huge Essex County parks in Newark, covers part of the old Fair Grounds. The New Jersey State Fair was conducted at Waverly for many years. The site was given the name by Mary Mapes Dodge.

Dressing warm and wearing goggles were essential when taking a ride in an open touring car.

Elsie Kolb (far left) and Matilda Fox (far right) join friends for a holiday swim.

The *Majestic*, an excursion boat, steams along the Passaic River.

Patrons crowd McGovern's Tavern at 58 New Street. The tavern was founded in 1936 by Frank J. McGovern, an Irish immigrant, when Prohibition ended. He organized the Frank McGovern Association to assist young immigrants and also initiated the St. Patrick's Day parade. The jukebox plays Irish tunes. Patrons still include new immigrants, faculty members from Rutgers-Newark, Essex County College, Seton Hall Law School, New Jersey Institute of Technology, and the University of Medicine and Dentistry, as well as personnel from the Essex County Court House.

Men play boccie, an Italian bowling-type game, in this photograph. A boccie court is in Branch Brook Park, Essex County's oldest park, which was developed by John Charles Olmsted, nephew and adopted son of Frederick Law Olmsted in 1896. Many other boccie courts were in backyards of Italian homes beside their grape arbors.

Three *Newark Evening News* photographers dressed up in top hats, canes, and tails to participate in a St. Patrick's Day parade *c.* 1966, after some good-natured kidding of each other. They are, from left to right, Tom Christie, Jack Johnston, and Dick Lowey.

Jerry Lewis, a graduate of South Side High School (Malcolm X Shabazz High School), continues to work as a comedian today.

Newark native Connie Francis, a popular singer and motion picture actress, presents flowers to her parents, Mr. and Mrs. George Franconero Sr., at a family celebration at Thomm's Restaurant on January 11, 1970.

Marty Ames, a saxophonist, was one of the most popular orchestra leaders in the Newark area. He played at many affairs at the YM-YWHA, as well as dinners and bar mitzvahs at temples and banquet halls.

Whitney Houston, a Newark native, is shown here singing at one of her concerts.

Claude E. Holgate, a sports writer for the *Newark Evening News*, a nature lover, painter, and president of the New Jersey Automobile Club, arranged the first automobile parade in Newark. This grew into the Bamberger's Thanksgiving Day parade.

Dore Schary, a film writer and director, was active in the Newark YM-YWHA. The Y drama groups featured many dramatic shows, concerts, and other events, and served as a training place for many potential entertainers.

Ten
Pride of Newark

Sir Thomas Lipton appears on
WOR Radio at L. Bamberger and
Company in October, 1922.

Stephen Crane, an internationally recognized poet and author, was born in Newark where his father, Rev. Jonathan Townley Crane, was a Methodist pastor. His novel *The Red Badge of Courage* changed the way people looked at the Civil War and war in general.

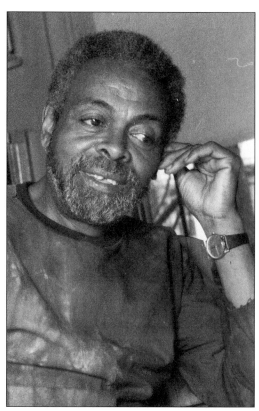

Amiri Baraka (the former LeRoi Jones), a poet and writer, is an activist for African-American causes in Newark.

Philip Roth (right), a graduate of the
Weequahic High School, talks with John
T. Cunningham, historian and former
Newark Evening News reporter, at a meeting
of the Friends of the Newark Library.
Roth is an outstanding novelist,
and Cunningham writes books on
New Jersey subjects.

Mary Mapes Dodge, who lived in the Lyons
Farms section, wrote *Hans Brinker; or The
Silver Skates* for her sons, who enjoyed ice
skating. She edited *St. Nicholas*, a magazine
for children, for many years.

Thomas Lynch Raymond was one of the city's most popular and progressive mayors. He spearheaded the development of Newark Airport, but died just two days before it was dedicated. Raymond Boulevard is named for him.

Meyer Ellenstein, the first Jewish mayor of Newark, served from 1933 to 1941.

Leo Carlin, president of the Teamsters Union (AFL), was elected to the City Commission in 1949 and advocated a change in government to a strong mayor-council. The change was made in 1954. Carlin served as mayor in 1953 and was reelected in 1954 and 1958. He was defeated when he sought reelection against Hugh Addonizio in 1962.

Kenneth Gibson (right) files his petitions for election as mayor with City Clerk Harry Reichenstein. He became the first African-American mayor.

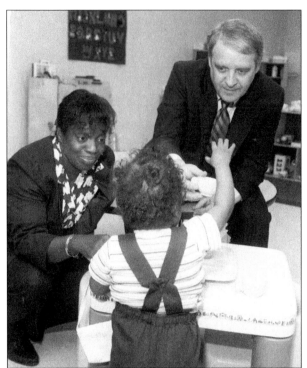

Mary Smith, executive director of Babyland, and State Senator Richard J. Codey chat with a toddler at the Babyland Nursery. The nursery is part of the facilities of New Community Corporation.

Inspecting plans for a senior citizen rehabilitation housing project on South Eighth Street, from left to right, are: Walter Johnson (area director of the HUD), William L. Johnston (executive director of New Jersey Housing Finance Agency), Rev. William L. Linder (member of the agency), and Albert Bradsher (president of the Roseville Senior Association). Rev. Msgr. Linder, then pastor of Queen of Angels Roman Catholic Church and now pastor of St. Rose of Lima Church, spearheaded the founding of New Community Corporation in 1968, with a Walk for Understanding.

Gaetano C. Cavicchia, son of Angelo, became
a professor of romance languages at Brown
University, Providence, Rhode Island, c. 1930.

Constance Woodruff, a community leader,
talks with A. Zachary Yamba, president of
the Essex County College.

Clement Alexander Price, a professor of history at Rutgers-Newark, has served as chairman of the New Jersey Council of the Arts. Price is considered to be an outstanding historian and has received many awards.

Assembly Speaker Dominick A. Cavicchia poses with his twelve-year-old son John after the senior Cavicchia was inaugurated as speaker on January 11, 1944. Mr. Cavicchia, a lawyer, served in the General Assembly from 1939 to 1944. As part of the installation ceremony, John was given an opportunity to strike the gavel. Mr. Cavicchia, a grandson of Angelo Cavicchia, was brought up by his uncle, Peter A. Cavicchia, who served as a congressman from 1931 to 1937.

Mr. and Mrs. James A. Coe share a book on their golden wedding anniversary at their High Street home.

This *c.* 1942 photograph shows members of the Calabrese family, including: (seated in front) Ralph (an architect with Frank Grad & Sons, Architects), Gloria (the youngest daughter), Virginia (his wife); (standing) Rose, Alfred, Daisy, Eddie, and Eleanor. Another son, Frank, was in the United States Army.

Sarah Vaughan, a popular jazz singer, was a Newark native.

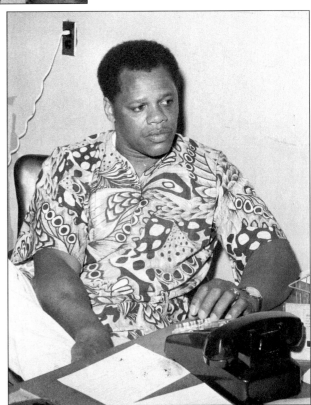

Milton Campbell, the 1956 Olympic decathlon champion, sits in the Milt Campbell Center, a recreation center which he operated at 187 Belmont Avenue (later renamed the Irvine Turner Boulevard) in Newark.

Sharpe James, now the mayor of the city, stands with his family on May 13, 1986, as he greets supporters at a rally at the Essex County College. Family members are, from left to right, his wife Mary, and his sons, John, Elliott, and Kevin.

In 1974, City Councilman Henry Martinez became the first Hispanic elected to the Newark City Council. Martinez was council president in 1986.

Donald M. Payne (on the left) talks with Ronald Rice at a City Council meeting. In 1988, Payne became the first African-American congressman from New Jersey.

William Ashby (seated at center) was honored on his birthday by members of the Newark Landmarks and Preservation Committee. They are: Elizabeth Del Tufo (seated at left) and standing, from left to right: Douglas Eldridge, Donald Dust, and Dr. E. Alma Flagg, assistant superintendent of schools. Mr. Ashby was the first director of the Urban League in both Elizabeth and Newark in 1916.

People crowd Ferry Street during a Portuguese Festival. Festivals and parades are featured by every ethnic group throughout the city.

Congressman Peter W. Rodino Jr. (1949–1989, on the right) stands beside a monument dedicated on June 27, 1976, to Peter Francisco, a Portuguese native, who served during the American Revolution. To the left of Rodino is John W. Francisco, great-grandson of Peter Francisco. The small park was renamed Francisco Park. It is located near the Penn Station.

IN HONOR OF
PETER FRANCISCO
THE HERCULES OF THE
AMERICAN
INDEPENDENCE

Richard T. Koles

Jean-Rae Turner